The Case

of the Restless Redhead

For Allen
with all best wishes
and gratitude for
your inspiration and
wisdom

Anne
May 2015

ALSO BY ANNE CARROLL FOWLER

Five Islands (chapbook, Pudding House)
Whiskey Stitching (chapbook, Pudding House)
Summer of Salvage (chapbook, Pudding House)
What I Could (chapbook, Pudding House)
Liz, Wear Those Pearl Earrings (winner of Frank Cat Press
Chapbook Contest)

The Case

of the Restless Redhead

Poems by

Anne Carroll Fowler

Antrim House
Simsbury, Connecticut

Library of Congress Control Number: 2015931973

ISBN: 978-1-936482-82-5

First Edition, 2015

Printed & bound by Mira Digital Publishing

Book design by Rennie McQuilkin

Front cover design and photograph ("The Crime Scene")
by Christopher Harris (www.chrisharrisphoto.com)

Photographs on pp. iii and 49 (crime scene photos)
are courtesy of the Maine Attorney General

Author photograph by Sharyn Peavey
(www.sharynpeavey.com)

Antrim House
860.217.0023
AntrimHouse@comcast.net
www.AntrimHouseBooks.com
21 Goodrich Road, Simsbury, CT 06070

In loving memory of my grandmother,
Anne Carroll (Nancy) Payson Holt

ACKNOWLEDGMENTS

I wish to thank the editors of the journals in which some of the poems in this volume first appeared, at times with different titles and in different versions:

2 River Review: "Those Xeroxed Pictures from the A.G's Office"

Common Ground: "Benjamin Payson Holt"

Larcom Review: "Granny Thought She Was Lucky" (as "Granny's Fingers")

Penwood Review: "Recess"

Pinyon Review: "Dusk," "Returning," "Who Can Tell Me"

Poetry, Memoir, Story: "Anne Carroll Payson Holt"

"Granny's Lawn in August," "Portrait of Benjie (as "Little Brother's Face"), "Red Dog (as "Hazard"), and "In the Cutting" (as "Tea Roses") were reprinted in the chapbook *Liz, Wear Those Pearl Earrings* (Frank Cat Press) where "After Benjie Was Born" (as "Sepia Family") also appeared.

"The Earliest Time (as "At Rocky Point") was reprinted in the chapbook *Five Islands* (The Pudding House Press).

"First Bullet Landed" (as "The Deep Green") appeared in the chapbook *Whiskey Stitching* (The Pudding House Press).

I am grateful to the Maine Attorney General, Janet Mills, and her staff for their help in providing crime scene photos as well as police and witness statements regarding my grandmother's case. Thanks also to the research staff at the Maine Historical Society, who helped me research my grandmother's early life.

And many thanks to my thoughtful, helpful, patient readers: Sam Allen, John Gibson, Addison Hall, Jep Streit, Geraldine Zetzel, and above all, Wendy Mnookin, Stephen Tapscott, Catherine Sasanov, and Barbara Helfgott-Hyett.

TABLE OF CONTENTS

III. AFTER

We die with the dying:
See, they depart, and we go with them.
We are born with the dead:
See, they return, and bring us with them.

– T. S. Eliot, "Four Quartets"

Death does not take the dead away; it only
makes them grow more deeply into us.

– Yiyun Li, "A Sheltered Woman"

THE CASE

OF THE RESTLESS REDHEAD

The Case of the Restless Redhead

The very first Perry Mason TV episode,
a real cliffhanger. The redheaded
dame (hair grey in black-and-white)
finds a strange snub-nosed gun in the cigarette box
on her coffee table. Of course she calls

Perry. Then, fleeing in her convertible
coupe, she's chased by a frightful figure
wearing a pillowcase with eyeholes, driving
a great finned Chevy, gesticulating wildly.
She fires the mystery pistol at him.

Now the police want her for murder!
When all *she* ever wanted was to be
a movie star. Perry doesn't quite trust her,
those big blue eyes. She does keep sighing,
lying, batting her improbable lashes at him.

Everybody smokes and drinks,
stays up all night. No one wears a seat belt.
Paul and Perry solve the puzzle of twin
Colt 38s, multiple aliases, get the bad guys
as they will each week, body after body,

September to May. All
the blood's kept out of sight.

I. THEN

Interrogation (1)

Do you hate them,
Leland and Fred and Ronnie?
I don't know them.
Do you hate them,
Immie and Denise and Cheryl?
The girls were so young.
Do you hate them?
It wasn't personal.
Do you hate them?
They were drunk.
Do you hate them?
They didn't plan to.
Do you hate them?

Dusk

Petal the dachshund walks with her
to the end of the road, to the mailbox.

Bills paid, winter coats
brought from the cedar closet.

Day of virtue, and now the smoky
Lapsang, with lace cookies, lemon,

sugar and silver tongs. The swooning
of gardenia in the south window

filling up the air. My grandmother breathes
the passing season. Before she

gets up with the tray, as doves
land on the eaves, as the gardenia

drops its blossoms, let the fox
run free in the field, let Petal

leap onto her lap, lick her face
all over

with that fierce tongue.

Last Call

I was curled in the black wicker chair
she bought me at the church auction, phone
sitting on the small side table she gave me,
neck cramped from clutching the receiver.

We talked about the party next week,
her eightieth birthday. *What
are you going to wear?* I told her
Lizzie had learned to say
her middle name, the name they shared.

I have dialed it back thirty years—my brick
and board bookshelves, late afternoon light,
west-facing windows. But did she call me *Pet*
as always? Did I say, *I love you?*

I've still got that table, piecrust trim
chipped and mended from all the times it's tipped over.
I can't quite remember her number—I know
it began with *seven. Seven…*

Ambulance: Three Ten A.M.

Her wedding ring, her scarab
bracelet trapped in a plastic bag.

If they had called me—
If they had thought—
I would have driven
through the night.

Maybe they
can't think. Maybe Mother
wants Granny to herself.

Our priest identifies her.
Dad keeps complaining
he's forgotten his glasses.

Is it me
lying on that cold table, bullet hole
through one blue eye?

What shape does death
leave on her face, on all
our faces?

Granny Thought She Was Lucky

          despite everything:
her baby Benjie dying,
brother John bankrupt
shooting himself in the heart,
brother Olcott drunk
killed in his car crash.

Despite my mother's
rejection of permanent
waves, the Colonial Dames.
Despite Grandpa.

She had a gift for finding
four-leaf clovers. She did, every time.
What's your secret? I asked her once.
I always look. I always look.

When those men
break in the window
she switches on the light,

gropes for her glasses,
for a future, reaching
for the phone, dragging

those holes around the dial.

Autopsy

Dr. Charles F. Branch,
Post Mortem Report

One's first impression
is that this lady
had auburn hair.

But rinse away
the stains. Wipe
away the dried
blood bathing
her whole
head and neck.
You find

this comely, slight,
elderly female
had curled
gold white hair
very well kept.

red sky at morning

sailors take   shake off   warning
cloud sprawl   flicker   right
returning   through   God's pity
spanfire   forbade   billow
bleed   marooned   wavespan
shipwrack   forbode   eyetrace
flame rags   refract   old wives
weatherghost   firepaint
firmament   mare's tail
haircurl   flashfire
skyblaze   lowering

On a Night Like Any Other

she sits up
slowly, eases her legs over the mattress,
grips the bedpost for balance, limps
to the cabinet, must take more pills

but starts
across the hall to check on Ben,
remembers—he's gone
to Ledgeview Nursing Home.
She must cream her face
with Oil of Olay, settle a hairnet
over her gold-white waves,
swallow pills, head for bed.

She's almost eighty, or eighteen
again, riding the bridle paths, sailing
down Casco Bay, fitting the green gown
for her debutante ball, packing the blue
fur-trimmed coat for college.

How it shrinks to habit,
necessity, intention—how
she must read more history,
join the Theology Club at St. Mary's.
She can't kneel now to say her prayers.

First Bullet Landed

       in Gus Peck's painting on her wall
right in the heart of the green.
Gus went back with Granny to the storied
days in Cleveland, bathtub gin, the Black Maria,
his girl with the botched abortion.

Later Gus would come to Maine each August,
paint bad watercolors in the mornings.
Afternoons he'd sit with Grandpa, holding
forth on Art, both of them holding
highball glasses. "The Deep Green"

the only decent painting
Gus ever made.

Room, House

1.

eyelashes drift downward,
eyelids endstop   *promised rooms*

soft skin slackens   cheeks,
jaws. Chin drops   *music*

of crystal spheres   heaven
of fixed stars   dwelling places.

Fingers grip and loosen
eyelet lace   *stations*   many,

way or missed   something not
returning   or The Cross   rest stop, stop

loss   if it were not so I would have...
imagined   prayed for   *mansions.*

2.

In my Father's house are many mansions.

3.

She is passing   through tea roses,
along the bridle path

while the night   unmakes tomorrow,
her handsome   soldier cutting

the wedding cake   with his sword,
her hand arresting   his wandering hand.

The morsel   of lead passed
through her   the drop of blood

on the sheet   Not enough
linen to soak it up.

red seeing

flashpoint   word fire   three again
throwing   spitfire
that napkin ring   bloodstir
your hair   Sally's muddy
coat   bills   barfights
a tantrum   throwing   matchfire
carrot top   ignite   wildcat
in air   wordblaze   or sudden
shoulder blossom   eyeburst
blame   endspot

The Perps

They steer the rubbished streets of South Portland
past oil tanks, freight yards, vacant lots
fenced with chain, cruising wasted asphalt
on the Million Dollar Bridge. The nights pour
into gallon jugs of cheap cocktails.

One voice pitched above the others,
a lame crow's, bossy, unhinged. A hazard fiddling
with a pen gun, fate no bigger than a finger.
Flooring it through a cemetery, firing

at gravestones, this small hard city.
Working up to who knows
what happens next.

The Day Before They Killed
My Grandmother

Their last ordinary day together—the girls
go to the Cherry Pie to get their nails done.
To celebrate. Denise is engaged to Fred!
With a ring to prove it, though where
he got it, *that's* a mystery. She doesn't care.
She does care. On parole for stickup and kidnapping
a policeman—*I know he needs me to go straight.*

Cheryl is almost 19, but Denise is more mature—
look, she got Fred, twice her age. Marching
down Congress toward the salon, arms linked,
teased hair staunch in the fall breeze. Even Immie
in a good mood. Busted two weeks ago for hooking,
now Immie's got Leland and—being a juvy—*a bitchin*
social worker. She'll keep my dumbass father off me.
Leland's an older man, too, he takes care of business.

In the Cherry Pie they scrutinize plastic racks
of gaudy polish, choose colors, paying close
attention to themselves. While they still can.

They Drive

the old Pontiac around a couple
of days. Guys in front, girls in back, all
drinking beer, coffee brandy with milk.
Leland shooting out the window
while he's driving, while Fred's driving.

How about that guy who scored some
stolen TVs off a boxcar. $50!
In West Falmouth, but no luck—
got no house numbers.
How about Old Lady Holt

in Falmouth? So down Route 88, past
the cemetery, through the open
iron gate, down the long dirt road, the
ruts and bumps, to the circular drive.
Girls, stay in the car!

Immie thinks they're coming to a party.
Stupid cunt. It started as a party. *Fred,*
get the tire iron from the trunk.
Girls, shut up! They look in the garage,
knock on the door. Walk around

side, everything dark. Pushing
through roses to the bathroom window.
Leland puts the gun between his teeth—
Gimme the tire iron—smashes glass.
Climbing in, careful of the shards.

Where Was Glenda
the Housekeeper?

Flinty
tobacco-chewing
Glenda

them knocking
at the backdoor

If she'd just
yelled *Go away*
hadn't locked
herself upstairs

If she'd appeared
in her nightgown
with her gun or
fired a shot
out her window

If she hadn't
called her sister
before 911

If she hadn't told
the dispatcher
they'd already gone—

What Were They Thinking?

That Denise said the old lady was sick
and mostly in bed, wouldn't know
at 11:00 P.M.? Wouldn't hear a breaking
window? That Glenda wouldn't call the police?

That they'd know a real old antique if they
saw one? That with six of them they'd be able to fit
a Queen Anne table, a Sheraton dresser
six feet tall, a Windsor chair into the car?

Hard Rain

Custom House Wharf after midnight. City
tug, harbor launch, fishing trawler
all moored to bollards. Sigh of bumpers
against the pier, ache and strain of line.
Then smack of a window flung up fast—second
floor—a rain of plunky splashes in the harbor:
TV, radio, four boots, a pair of sneakers.
A spring two inches long. Something shaped
like a cigar. Lover's quarrel?
Angry wife? Nobody's business.

II. BEFORE

Who Can Tell Me

where Granny and Grandpa met?
The Portland Country Club—
two golfing parties halted at the sand trap?
A debut ball at the old Falmouth Hotel?
Or crossing Harvard Yard? A law student
spit-polished in Army uniform?
An eager theatre pupil, pompadour
ablaze in autumn sun?
Or blame her brother Charley,
the ladies' man—maybe he introduced
them. Did Ben see the steely set
of her jaw? Nancy notice
the pint flask belted at his hip?
But I lose the story. Married
1917. Her father would never
have countenanced an actress
in the family. Her second ambition
was to be swept away by love.

Granny Writes to Her Future Husband

Ben Dearest, we are translating the play *Phormio*
in Latin class, all full of terrible
idioms. The Prof said, *One would know
Darius is a slave by his red wig.*

Then she saw my head in the sun,
heard a few giggles. Oh, all the girls
found this great fun!
Not that the Romans thought red curls

menial, the Prof hastily explained.
Oh no! They thought them very very handsome.
But slaves had light hair, as they came
from foreign lands, different from dark Romans.

Oh yes! Very beautiful! Honestly
I almost laughed out loud.
Imagine, apologizing to me —
as if red hair wasn't perfectly proud!

The Earliest Time

The fog's insatiable this morning, devours
boats at anchor, Basket and Clapboard
Islands, the Bay. Spits out morsels
for my foraging eye. Hammering sounds
up Mill Creek—somebody building
an invisible house. I know what else
I can't see—that deep thrum's
the *Nancy H,* hauling traps beyond the Point.
Somewhere, a great blue heron,
that edgy question mark, stalks
the shallows. On Ten Pound Island,
the ruined boathouse where Granny's
brothers played poker and drank whiskey
after dinner. No women allowed.
Did they play by candlelight? Play
till dawn? The next big storm will
flatten the place. But now, the living surge!
The sun up there, burning the fog
into a whiteness bright as new paint
on the *Nancy H,* bright as yesterday,
or the heron's eye as he lunges
after one silver streak, another.

Red Dog

1.

Nancy's painted her toenails green,
gold flecked. They're sailing west
in the blue sloop *Desperado,* all her brothers,
her new husband, playing poker as they scud

across Penobscot—red dog, five card stud,
up and down the river—drinking bootleg
from Ben's silver flask. Small islands
mirage in the distance. She doesn't know
yet what hand she's picked.

2.

Ben places his glass of gin and bitters
on the stone wall, with both hands grasps
a phantom club. He's chipping, pitching,
bending an iron shot around a tree, over
and over swinging at the invisible ball—*discipline*—

eyes fixed on club's arc, ball's dimpled surface,
its arc across the field, into the churchyard. *Hole in one!*
He stoops, pockets unseen tees. He'll head over
to the Club, pick up a game, a gimlet, a girl.

Husband

She convinced herself there was nothing
but him—no untraceable flares
or un-plucked strings. No unscrubbed

hearts or bodies to know. Her restive hair?
His bauble. A bob. So she slides into wife-
dom. Dominion. Silk shirts, silk

kisses. But then the mess of it. Kisses spilt,
creditors' clamors. Begging. *Mother, dearest,*
a small loan for a new Easter hat?

Maine to Cleveland

Let the sun through Pullman windows

soothe, clack of wheel on track erase.
In the breakfast car, let the lady from Memphis

offer, *When husbands are asleep at least
we know where they are.*

Let Ben appear, not natty, muttering
hair-of-the-dog, heading for the bar.

The engineer's not right either. Beyond
Pittsburgh, screeching, iron

on steel, shudder, full crashing
stop. Two tires, a man's torso

hurtle past the window, fall in full
view to the embankment. Hours'

delay for police to clear the track
of mangled car, two dead. Let the next

engineer deliver the newlyweds
to the new city, their frontier,

his chance to become his own man.

Cleveland, 1919

Her first time
handling an iron
she finishes Ben's
one silk shirt
to perfection, buttons it
for him Easter morning.
He snaps cufflinks
in place, then slips
them out again, rolls
his sleeves. *Damn it!*
I'd rather scullery
than church!
He wears her sweater
to protect the shirt,
picks up the duster.
She fixes her new hat
with a pin. If only
Father could see
Ben now
so industrious!

red paint the town

Hell, I'm not going to arrest nobody
for doing what I like to do myself.
Cleveland Policeman, 1919

a little hair of   cupie bow
the dog   dressing up   moonshine
stepping out   roll those stockings
down   electric   three cent fare
glitter   damn Volstead   midnight
speakeasy   first red scare   slip
a sawbuck   raids   pass on by
cloche hats   zozzled   May Day Riots
home rule   velvet rope   crooners
Bugsy!   boogie-woogie   paddy
wagon   Roaring 20s   home

First Born

Not a son. A daughter, Sally.
Not sugar and spice,

another redheaded
restlessness.

Raucous plump, brown-
sweatered gnome

an ambitious horse…
A too-tiny house.

I left my coat in the hotel
but at least it wasn't the baby.

Random damage
to the dining room—

Naughty girl!
Thank God for

Beulah, so black
Sally calls her *Ink*!

After Benjie Was Born

They arranged themselves—you can almost
see quotation marks floating in the air—
on the cast iron bench at the edge of the lawn,
backs to Casco Bay. Ben in white flannels,
saddle shoes, customary cross-legged pose—

his languid hazardous hand. Nancy's bob
lacquered against the breeze, strappy
sandals pricking the lawn like tees.
She presents little Benjie like Baby Jesus,
tells her daughter, *Sit up straight!*

But before the photographer can click the picture
Sally stares off, moony, to the left. Looks beyond
the empty wooden ladder-back. Her legs spread.
Wide floppy satin bow fades into pale sky.
A sepia family, no one's missing. So why the extra chair?

Sally Comes Downstairs
for School

Her father happens over
and over: always

in the wing chair
in the parlor, always still

in evening clothes, nose
bloody or eye blooming:

a car crash
happens, a speakeasy

brawl, cleaned out
at poker. While her mother

tries to happen
herself: a bag of ice, a glass

of bitters and soda. It all fits
but not quite right. And Sally

happens to be late. *Lazy girl…*
missed breakfast. Hurry off now.

Benjamin Payson Holt,
1927–1929

He will always be
a white wraith,
copper-curled, barely
able to walk, a flannel
doll against Beulah's
huge blackness.
It wasn't his birth,
not even his death,
but the in between:
unrelenting
colic, eczema,
the black ointment—
think of it,
a baby
with aluminum mittens
on his poor hands
so he can't scratch
oozing sores!
How to forgive
Sally carrying death?
Or Ben,
who never
stepped inside
the nursery? How to
forgive
her heart
kneeling before
his casket in shamed
gratitude, in
inconsolable relief?

Portrait of Benjie

      floats in a gilt frame
above the mantel: angelic eyes,
round collar of his blouse
appliquéd with tulips.
Sally rests on Mother's chintz *chaise longue*
memorizing his immaculate
cheeks, smile, tries spitcurling
her strawberry bangs.

      If she hadn't
brought home whooping cough
he'd be here now, playing
lead soldiers under
the piano, swinging on drapes
in the drawing room, losing
at dominoes.

      Now maybe
Mother will take her
riding, to the talkies,
to live in Maine
all year. She could learn
tennis at the Club.

      But if her case
had been more serious
maybe *she* would be displayed:
green smocked dress,
holding her kitten Snowdrop,
roses all around her,
framed in gold
behind velvet ropes
at the Art Museum.

Hybrid Teas

After Benjie dies, Nancy's prayers go in every
direction, or none. Her father takes charge, builds
her the house she wants, down the lane
from the family's summer place.

She designs it: long pine-paneled living room, azure
cathedral ceiling, French doors overlooking the Bay.
What if loss is not accident, test, but destiny,
God's bland intention. John Larsen,

her mother's gardener, builds a dry-stone wall
to fence out the meadow. She grows tea roses
beneath her windows—*Queen o'the Lakes,*
Mischief, Maiden's Blush. She grafts a hybrid,

a light russet, names it *Heart's Tears.*

Portrait of My Grandfather

Seated in an unlikely chair—a lady's
upholstered vanity—my grandfather
holds his head in one hand, droops
the other over his crossed knee.

His habitual *langueur*. He's dressed
in a three-piece suit. On the floor
by his feet, a book half read,
a highball glass half empty.

Next year they'll move
to Manhattan. A decade later
back to Maine for good, after
he's let go by his law firm.

She'll join The Colonial Dames,
become president of Country
Women of the World. He'll be
a failed gentleman farmer.

No one asks why or what he did.
No one says New York's
a big place to have to leave.

In the Cutting

                garden,
John Larsen stakes
    delphinium, gladioli.
Blunt fingers coax
    and marshal beauty.
  He manages Nancy's flowers,
    all but her precious roses.

Sally plays hide-and-seek
    with herself down
        in the sunken garden.
Drags a broken
    branch along the wall.
That child makes more noise
    than the bulls of Bashan.

On the sidelawn, Ben swings
    at an unseen ball—
        address position, full body coil,
    pivot, right side
        release.

Across the field, church bells
    sound for Evensong.
Across the field little Benjie
    lies in St. Mary's churchyard.
Nancy thinks of roses, roots
    embracing underground.

Stop Getting Married

Granny says, after my second husband
leaves. *But what about Mimi—married
five times?*

*Oh, Mimi, she married men she met
on airplanes! You can choose,* she tells me,
*know lots of men, or know one
really well.* She gazes—her inscrutable look—
at Grandpa resplendent

photographed in World War One uniform,
sword belted at his side. *Once a man wanted me
to leave Ben and marry him,* she confides.
*But I could never do that to your mother.
And you must never tell her.*

Of course I told. *Oh, I remember
that guy,* mother says. *A doctor. Mother never
would have married him. He would have taken charge.*

Granny's Lawn in August

In the shade under ancient birches
Gus Peck and Grandpa, wrapped
in laprobes, drink tequila at three P.M.
My daughter Lizzie eats fistfuls of grass.
Granny's inside, making iced tea.
Beyond the wall three stout cows
graze in the sultry meadow.

Gus fuzzily reviews his theory
of perspective. Grandpa explains
the third tee at the Club. The French
door opens: Granny carries
a lacquered tray,
lemon sliced transparent,
silver tongs for lump sugar,
madeleines and zwieback.

Lizzie chews a lemon slice, stares
into her own dimension. She can't see
the cows over the wall. Granny lifts her,
and Gus, in a lucid moment—*Maybe
when she grows up she will remember
this very afternoon, this moment.*

Renovation

When does she know that she must move him? After
fifty years, the slow unwinding of their tangled life.

No longer rising from bed, only lying in his brown
wool dressing gown, calling for another vodka gimlet.

He greets his great-granddaughter Lizzie with—*mewling
and puking in the nurse's arms*—fragment of a ruined mind.

And Nancy's friend Gertie, bony body torqued with arthritis,
tongue like a darning needle, pats his knee

with a blotched, lascivious hand. *Ben and I
have such a strong attraction,*

but of course it's only sexual.
After he's settled at Ledgeview

she goes to visit. He calls her Mama. *But I'm
your wife!—Hell and damnation,* he tells her.

When she gets home she calls the painters.
She'll do his bedroom over in *Old Rose.*

Glenda

            the housekeeper, deserts her
housework, builds a scarecrow, dresses him—
old stalker hat and houndstooth coat—
like Sherlock Holmes! Hangs soap
in cheesecloth bags to keep the deer away.
She makes a slingshot from a crotched
oak branch and bungee cord, spends hours
perched on the wall—oversized
garden gnome shooting crows.
Evenings, she's skittery as a bedbug—how
to keep critters away all night? Sets
leg traps, catches a raccoon, two groundhogs,
and a porcupine. One morning it's the mother
fox trying to gnaw off her foot. *Too bad for her kits,*
Glenda says, *but she's a goner with that leg,*
and right off gets her .22.

Granny Lamenting

Cook Emma in her grave, John Larsen too crippled
to care for himself, let alone prune hedges.

Glenda dusts fecklessly, smokes small cigars,
guards her vegetables: *flowers are useless*!

Some ladies have begun wearing trousers in town.
Ragtag friends of the houseboy park cars in her drive,

kick threadbare tires, mooch around drinking beer.
Don't they have jobs? The shutters need painting.

The housegirl Denise scorches the linen.
No one even remembers cigarette caddies.

Foghorn

She studies herself in the matching mirrors,
concave, convex. In one she balloons,
in the other shrinks, a pinprick
of plum wool. No one dies

of loneliness. She'll wear
her new blue suit to church,
take lunch at the Club.
She'll go for a color rinse and perm.

What makes a heroine?—Anna
lying on train tracks, Hedda Gabbler
seizing the gun? She'll hold on
to her view of Mussel Cove, compose
her own story, draw the drapes,
hold a match to the fire.

Portraits of My Grandmother

Mine posed, stunning in her flapper phase, stiff
on an iron garden settee with Grandpa Ben:
indolent, dandified, golf club dangling
from his index finger.

Beautiful still at eighty, no loss or compromise
traced on her face. Captured in lavender silk,
leaning toward the camera, Granny salutes
my brother on his wedding day,
willing him blessings.

Now she presides over my front hall,
monumental, auburn-haired in a lime green gown.
Is that you? everyone asks. *My grandmother,
my namesake,* I tell them, taking another bite
of vanity, that wormy apple.

red rover

come over
come over

III. AFTER

Interrogation (2)

Do you hate them?
Why did they have to?
Do you hate them?
She'd just moved Grandpa.
Do you hate them?
She was not at all sick!
Do you hate them?
She was just starting.
Do you hate them?
She was going to Australia!
Do you hate them?
We had to cancel her party.
Do you hate them?
I was named for her.
Do you hate them?

Regarding Holt Murder

South Portland Police Report 10/5/76

The undersigned officer
observed a vehicle
operating on Broadway
occupied by several subjects.

Activities within
included subjects
looking back at cruiser.

Olive green in color,
1970 Ford Galaxie
two-door hardtop, color
faded and unkept [sic]*.*

Operator identified
as Frederick C. Askew
of Portland, Maine,
extremely nervous.
Askew overly cooperative,
by explanations without questions.

Male subjects were read
their rights. Questioned
if they understood.
Each one given
a pat down search.

Askew carring [sic]

a large pocketknife.
Search of vehicle
found a silver tray, one tire iron
under the passenger seat.

Trunk in disarray:
two tire irons
dirty and rusted.

Upon examination
Fred Askew's left hand
showed a small narrow cut,
smeared blood. Leland Roy's hand
showed dirt and grease,
a small blister burn wound.

Most of the occupants
had criminal records. Were released.
The silver tray: retained
by the South Portland Police.

Those Xeroxed Pictures from
the A.G.'s Office

show everything in her bedroom
as I remember—*chaise longue* covered
in pink and green flowered chintz,

matching curtains, tall dark mahogany bureau,
mirrored dressing table, pastels of two ethereal
children over the mantel. The cane she hated,

hooked on the cannonball-and-carved-
bell headboard. Her bed table: lamp
with its ruffled shade, big rotary

phone, strand of pearls, open book
upside down. Her balloon spectacles,
frames band-aid-colored. The ones she needed

to read the phone. A silver-handled
magnifying glass, porcelain ashtray, a half-
smoked cigarette. These last pictures: look

at them. The unmade bed, dark-
stained sheets and laid across
the bedspread, somehow, her

bloody lacy cotton gown.

Holed Up

Their sad address near the scrap metal yard,
the Coastguard station. Two-family bungalow,
Ronnie and Cheryl on one side, Leland—his
blistered hand—on the other. Immie coming,

going. Shag carpets, gritty, stained. Couple
of mildewed cushions on the sagging couch.
Ragged nods and fingernails. Two weeks.
Immie with fast food, plastic and styrofoam piling up.

One story takes up all the room. How
to tell it, rehearsing, each of them,
over and over, threatening, matching,
shouting, getting every detail right.

If only, if only. Cigarette ash in the sink.
Panic of passing black-and-whites. Foghorns
and spilt milk, the smelly fridge. Immie wailing
through the walls, *What about me?*

After dark, to Evelyn's Tavern
for a drink. *Where's Fred and Denise?*
The tab Leland's run up
that can never be paid.

Cheryl Breaks First

Party girl, weak link, scared
of everything: fog, police, shadow, but finally
hell or Leland—maybe they're the same. That
old music unraveling. Somebody else's
party now. Ronnie's a chicken, a snitch, but
his hands are cleanest. Cheryl's fifth grade cursive:
Leland make a comment, "might have to get
rid of a piece." Her crude drawing of a gun.
It look like a cigar.

No Mendelssohn, no confetti, but Denise
marries in front of the coffee machine
in the Portland Police Jail. No bare skin,
nobody to stand up but the Sheriff. On that night
of everything Fred cries in bed. How can she not
love him? He's so deep, he reads books, needs her
more than ever. *Mrs. Frederick C. Askew, a bride*
of four days may spend the traditional honeymoon
next week as a prosecution witness in her husband's
murder trial.

Leland won't talk so Immie can't.
A chatterbox, all sass and spunk.
Now her greedy music's shut up,
her black cascade of curls chopped off.
Just seventeen, wrapped so tight and spoiling,
spoiled for hope, just glimpsing
that unyielding and murdered future
men can't save her from, men won't.

Fred and the Psychiatrist

Request for Psychological Consultation
Dr. E. Kron, 11.3.76

Evaluate mental state. Held for county
  Nailed on the Holt thing
murder charge. Attorney Stearns. Has previous
  In the Pen at Thomaston
history. Now on Parole.
  Looking at a long jolt this time
Asleep in his cell but quickly alert.
Bearded, well-nourished, muscular
  Miss my workouts, brother
white male. Not psychotic.
  Fuck I'm not crazy
Admits to occasional depression but talks
  I get down sometimes, man, but who don't?
realistically about that.
  What do I do? Get shitfaced
Above average intelligence. Has just read
  That guy Frankl's book
about concentration camp survival and
  Man, I can relate
no mental disorder.
Advise attorney not to prolong
  How long in this shithole?
in that location if possible.
Follow up again.

Leland

The cipher lurking
at the heart.
        No police statement.
        No psych eval.
        No testimony.

Fred says he said,
        I had to do it,
        I had to do it.

Cheryl says he said,
        Tell anyone about this
        I'll blow your heads off your shoulders.

Ronnie says he said
        Do you care about your parents?
        If I killed once I can do it again.

red fox

in the gulley   wary as
a creeper   among weedstalks
hunker   ears stiffen
in hollows   blaze of   bared
teeth   rusty points   restless over-
tracking   squat among   husks
white-tipped   thickets of   crunch
underground   shapeshift   stumphole
crouch   sacred fur   masked
in gloaming   stalk   supple flank
shadow sly   fire stealer   picking
through crickets   bite   dawn
rustle   dusk   familiar   gnaw

Telling Lizzie

We sit on the loveseat Granny gave me.
We talk. *We won't see Granny anymore…No, not*
Petal either…We won't go to her house…Sure
we can watch Mr. Rogers.

I think I've done such a good job.
I take her to the cemetery.
Lizzie thinks Granny's living underneath
the gravestone, with furniture and the dog

—a female pharaoh buried
with her full set of Rose Medallion china, necklace
with seventeen teardrop opals, little Benjie's portrait,
and Petal the dachshund, placid for once at her feet.

Before the Trial

Mother and I clean out all
the closets, drawers, retrieve
Petal from the police.

Are you ever going to cry?

I don't know. Maybe
after the trial. Maybe
after your grandfather dies.

We pack up his army
uniform, his tuxedo. What if
he'd still been home,

come out of his bedroom
wielding the sword?

First Day in Court

We sat in the tiered middle section, three rows back.
Mother, Dad, our priest, and me.
The defendants below us at a long table.
Both in suits. Gone is Leland's Fu Manchu moustache,
Fred's long bushy beard.

All day police—Portland, South Portland,
Falmouth—testify. Young men, longhaired,
sinister, fill one row of spectator seats.

The killers' friends, Mother guesses.
I ask the D.A. at a break. *Students at the Law School—
a murder trial—can't miss this opportunity!*

Over drinks that night Dad tells us he won't
be going back: *I don't like the way
I feel in there. I want to kill them.*

Testimony (1)

Fred called to the witness stand
swears to tell the whole truth and nothing but.
Says *Leland broke the window with the tire iron.*
Says *We climbed in. The bathroom.*

Says *I went into her bedroom*
heard her sit up. Sound of sheets.
Heard her turn on the light
gasp.

Says *I sat down on her bed*
and told her I'm sorry we did
wrong, I'll pay to get the window fixed.

Says she said *"Yes indeed it is wrong.*
I'm going to call the police.
Please hand me the phone.
Hand me my glasses."

Says *Then Leland came in,*
the glass cracks behind her head.
Says *Leland ran out then in again.*
Has to reload.

"My god I've been hit."
Leland runs out, back in again.
I hear the third shot
point blank.

Everyone in the courtroom
shifts on the benches.
The D.A. says, *Are you telling me
this elderly woman talked to you like that?*
The judge asks, *Is that a question, Counselor?*
Mother sighs.
They didn't know Granny, did they?

Testimony (2)

Ronnie says, *I never
went in.* Then says he did. Leland first,
then Fred, then him.

Fred says *I stayed in the bathroom.
Maybe the living room. Didn't see
a thing. Saw Leland with a bullet
in his teeth. Never went into the bedroom.*

Fred says…*a nightmare, a hand extending
over the footboard…a sound like a firecracker…
over her eye a bluish hole appearing…*

Leland says nothing.

Recess

Day 1

I follow Leland out. He's escorted down the hall
to a closet. He sits outside, smoking, guarded
by officers. I stand by the barred
window twenty feet away. Stare.

Day 2

Follow. Stand. Stare. When he notices, mark
his look, predatory, sexual. He might be
handsome, I don't know. He wants me. He
killed my grandmother. Hold his stare.

Day 3

Follow. Stand. Stare. He watches me
watch him smoke. Does he fathom
who I am? He shot her three times.
Keep staring.

Day 4

Did he see her pictures
in the *Portland Press Herald*? He wipes
a fleck of Camel ash off his lower lip,
looks around, looks down. Looks away.

Day 5

He folds himself forward, edges his chair back
toward the closet. I wrap her cashmere shawl
around me, lock my eyes on the black
of his bent head, catch his eyeshot glances.

Day 6

Chair's inside the closet. He enters that unlit
space, sits down, whispers to the officers.
They close the door. Arms stitched
to my chest. Stare at the door.

Day 7

Stare at the closed door. Is he glaring
from the other side? Sitting alone,
thinking Leavenworth or worse? In one
square yard of dark, smoking.

Day 8

He didn't take her opal necklace, insured
for fifty thousand dollars. Only the cheap
TV he ditched in Portland Harbor.
Stare at the scarred door.

Day 9

Keep to my station. Outside the hall window,
snowmelt on brick sidewalk, sky somewhere,
birds wheeling down. My thumb knuckle
bleeds where I've bitten hard.

Day 10

Concluding arguments. Judge's instructions.
Jury deliberates five hours. *Guilty.*
He never testified. But out in that hall, I did.
Staring.

I Dream of Fred

I do recall seeing a small dog there that was in the bedroom barking, but I didn't pay any attention because it was small.

Fred's statement to Portland Police

He throws himself over her.
Old woman's body
under his young hardness.
Saving her?
Fate is cruel, he says,
random even.
He rolls in the blood
and it's his. Mad drinking
days into mad drunken dogs into
his dark blood drying in her hair
into a dog so small
Fred takes her home.
And they never catch us.

No Matter

       how often I read yellowed clippings
from the *Portland Press Herald*, the *Evening Express;*
police reports, their repetitious discrepancies,
false leads they followed, witness statements—typed
or hand-written, Palmer Method or block print,
atrocious spelling; post mortem report's clinical detail
(massive hemorrhage from right axillary region);
psych reports and legal appeals. No matter how long I stare
at black and white photos (disheveled bedroom,
shattered bathroom window), I can't stop them drinking
Allen's Coffee Brandy, getting in the car.
They keep coming. They are always coming.

Returning

The house still calls out to me
        across the meadow
                where cattle once grazed.
        Across decades
new owners, renovations. Tea roses still
        blooming under the bedroom
windows, crimson shutters,
        their pine tree cutouts
                and the gulley
where the fox kept her kits. I stand in the dusty
        road, beyond the stonewall,
no longer welcome, still so poor
        for the loss of her,
her soft freckled arms
        open. I can see across
to the Bay, blue, opening, three white sails,
        horizon blurry today,
sky, sea exchanging. I come here,
        waking and sleeping, the landscape
always shifting to love.

        Somewhere in lush light
my grandmother's walking
        in green August.
Bees in clover,

dragonflies darting.
She takes the farm track
        dusty and rutted.
Past the old cowbarn,
        the low polo stables.

Cicadas and crickets
        are warning of autumn,
but not yet! She swings
        with her cane at the blue
iron standpipe; it rings out.
        She comes down the path
to the teahouse perched
        on the banking, stops
at the top of the stairs
        to the rock beach.
She could almost
        touch the cumulus
pillowing down the Bay.
        She calls to me.
Come out of the sun now.
        Come up to the house.
Come in, have a glass of tea.

FULL TEXT OF COMMENT BY JANET T. MILLS, MAINE ATTORNEY GENERAL

Cold blooded murder with pen gun on Bramhall Road, October, 1976.

Who could kill a 79-year old grandmother in her own home, in her own bed? Who could steal her life for a TV and a radio, useless loot dumped in the ocean in dark of the night? Who could shoot her in the eye with a "pen gun," an innocent-looking thing pretending to be a scribe's tool but used instead as an instrument of death, propelling a tiny bullet through an innocent eye, darkening her vision, stealing her life, leaving its signature of powder burns on her face, a "single-shot pen gun shaped like a magic marker," its blowback leaving a telltale blister on the criminal's hand?

One man already on parole for armed robbery and kidnapping, another picked up on weapons charges days after the murder. "I had to do it. I shot her," the ringleader told his friends back in the car. Not a game of Clue but the real life end of a real life, a senseless tragedy, the kind of crime we read about in the newspapers, headline grabbers that lapse the next day, next week, next year, out of our consciousness.

But what about the family and friends of Anne Payson "Nancy" Holt? What shock do they still feel, what memories and terrors do they still harbor? Our lives are not lived alone, nor do our deaths occur in a vacuum. In this volume, one fond family member has taken up the stylus, putting true pen to paper to memorialize one terrible event in the life of a Maine community done with a gun that pretended to be a pen.

Listen to her voice. Learn from these lines.

ABOUT THE AUTHOR

The Reverend Anne Carroll Fowler is an Episcopal priest, spiritual director and pastoral counselor in Portland, Maine. Her work has appeared in many journals, and is included in several anthologies. Four of her chapbooks have been published by Pudding House, and a fifth won the Frank Cat Press 2002 Chapbook Contest. For ten years she ran the Chapter & Verse Reading Series in Jamaica Plain, Massachusetts.

This book is set in Garamond Premier Pro, which had its genesis in 1988 when type-designer Robert Slimbach visited the Plantin-Moretus Museum in Antwerp, Belgium, to study its collection of Claude Garamond's metal punches and typefaces. During the mid-fifteen hundreds, Garamond—a Parisian punch-cutter—produced a refined array of book types that combined an unprecedented degree of balance and elegance, for centuries standing as the pinnacle of beauty and practicality in type-founding. Slimbach has created an entirely new interpretation based on Garamond's designs and on compatible italics cut by Robert Granjon, Garamond's contemporary.

To order additional copies of this book
or other Antrim House titles, contact the publisher at

Antrim House
21 Goodrich Rd., Simsbury, CT 06070
860.217.0023, AntrimHouse@comcast.net
or the house website (www.AntrimHouseBooks.com).

•

On the house website
in addition to information on books
you will find sample poems, upcoming events,
and a "seminar room" featuring supplemental biography,
notes, images, poems, reviews, and
writing suggestions.